A PASSION FOR CHINA

A PASSION FOR CHINA

A Little Book About the Objects We Eat From, Live With and Love

 molly hatch

september

Let me sit here for ever
with bare things,
this coffee cup,
this knife, this fork,
things in themselves,
myself being myself.
—

Virginia Woolf
The Waves

molly
hatch

For my daughter Camilla

INTRODUCTION

As we move through our daily lives, casually eating breakfast, sipping a leisurely afternoon cup of tea or gathering for a family dinner, the patterned ceramic objects we live with are precious witnesses to our stories. We eat from them, they warm our hands after a cold walk outdoors, we pull them out to celebrate the births, marriages and lives of our loved ones, we sometimes drop them carelessly or smash them in anger, and then we work to delicately glue them back together. Their familiarity becomes a part of our sense of ourselves, a sense of our home.

This book began because I wanted to revisit and learn more about the china I loved in my childhood. Where did the pieces come from? Who had them before my grandmother? What provenance has been lost that I could regain? If these objects could talk, what stories would they tell?

Looking at the family china, full of memory and meaning to me personally, drove me back to the museums where I first studied. As a young artist, I had relished these beautiful objects in museums, and had studied them within their walls, but I realized I needed to step back and research more in order to truly appreciate what ceramics have meant in human history. Only then could I appreciate the china from my own family history.

The story of how porcelain travelled from East to West is a fabulous one. The museums gave me tales of Queens and Kings, world travellers and explorers and even indentured servitude, and ultimately an understanding behind our collective love of porcelain.

Museums are the keepers of our larger histories. They record provenance, keep strangers' stories and select the objects worthy of study. In creating this book I was reminded that one is never too experienced to learn or too professional to be surprised by the past and how it can inform our present.

Tracing my role as a maker and designer in the lineage of studio potters in the Arts and Crafts movement gave me a chance to illustrate some of the most beautiful, formative studio pottery of the twentieth century.

But, in the end, the journey this book took me on was circular. In the last chapter we return to childhood; to the popular ceramics that inhabit our memories, that laid down an appreciation of colour and pattern in so many of us, and which are still used today.

From the clarity of blue and white to the tangled charm of floral patterns it was here that our passions for porcelain began. A passion that brings joy, but also exploration and knowledge. A never-ending relationship between the handmade, their makers and their holders; the past, the present and the future.

Molly Hatch
Massachusetts
2017

Chapter 1

Grandmother's House

THE THINGS
THAT SHAPED ME

My early childhood was spent on an organic dairy farm in Vermont. My parents were back-to-the-land hippies, following a sustenance living model for the majority of my youth. It was a pretty simple childhood — lots of days spent outside, working in the vegetable garden, hauling buckets of water to the animals, feeding baby calves from a bottle, making hay over long hot summers. For the most part, nature and animals were my playmates, the river across the street provided endless hours of entertainment for me and my brother. Life on the farm was largely about being outside. There were many

days hauling and stacking square hay bales onto the back of my father's Chevy truck with the promise of a ride on top of the stack from the field to the hay barn, plus the reward of a cold root beer soda from 'the store' at the end of the day (a rare treat in our house — there was only one general store to purchase food from in our tiny town). There were days weeding in the gardens and even more days harvesting food. I remember one summer in particular when I convinced my parents to grow shell peas by promising to personally shell all the peas myself so that I could have them to eat all winter (they were my favourite vegetable and too expensive to buy from the shop).

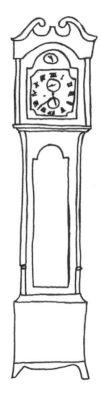

We lived in a large farmhouse built in the 1700s or 1800s. It was the classic clapboard-sided white farmhouse, rambling with additions over the years. The house was big enough that we lived only in one part of it during the winter, not bothering to heat the back half. It was full of furniture that my parents had acquired from their parents. My mother's relatives originally descended from an upper class family and most of the objects I grew up with were inherited from her side. So in many ways our life inside our house was in contrast to our life on the farm. We had silver to eat with, fancy china, a Victorian red velvet couch and even a grandfather clock. Summers were largely spent outside preparing for long winters inside. My mother found time to paint in the winter and there was time for sewing projects; generally a sense of leisure was associated with the indoors as well as the objects I grew up with — compared to time spent outdoors, which for me involved chores on the farm and for my parents was their work.

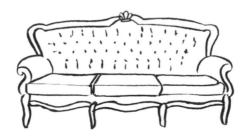

I have many clear memories of the objects I grew up with. I loved the drawers in the Spanish Bargueño writing chest in our living room, which stored lots of little things. I adored sorting through my mother's jewelry and playing with the French faience powder puff that elicited visions of eighteenth-century white wigs and princesses. I particularly loved going to my grandmother Myma's house, where she had a piano, marble lions and huge silver Repoussé mirrors, and where she painted in her studio all day. I thought my mother was crazy for not wanting to live like my grandmother — why work on a farm when you could paint all day instead? I aspired to achieve Myma's lifestyle ... so I studied my grandmother, visited often, talked with her about her life and, in those visits, studied the objects she owned. Sometimes I would even clean her house in an effort to study it. I polished her silver, or vacuumed the living room and dusted the artwork. Much of my interest in ceramics, particularly of the eighteenth century, has stemmed from the objects in my grandmother's home.

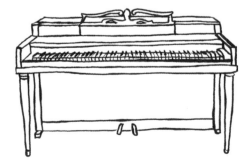

Working on this book has reintroduced me to the objects I have chosen to share with you. As I gathered images of the objects I remembered from my grandmother's home and even from museums, I came to realize that my memory of them wasn't always correct, and often had more to do with a sense of place and a period of time — or even a person. In this way so many objects we live with become animate parts of our family stories and our individual narratives — and, for me, my story as an artist and designer as well. Each object holds its own tale and has seen whole generations come and go. Yet these ceramic objects continue, standing witness to so much, and it is hard not to feel connectivity to the people who owned them before me. Researching the objects more, learning about the time periods they are from and even who made them and for whom and why only adds to my love for these objects.

Saucer

I don't know much about where this little saucer came from, but it was part of a larger set with teacups that went with it. I remember having tea parties with them when friends came over, as a little girl. This pattern has long been a favourite in my parents' house and this is the last one remaining after all the others have broken. It is chipped on the rim from my father using it a lot — he covers his mug with this saucer, keeping his morning tea hot while it is brewing. I love the little vignette of the house — or perhaps it is a church in the landscape. It is unusual to see a tin-glazed piece with just green and black decoration. It appears to be made in the delft fashion — with a red earthenware clay covered with a white tin glaze and hand-painted brushwork, although the Dutch delft pottery tradition is blue and white. I like that you can see the red clay beneath where the saucer has chipped. It looks like it was painted fast, with sure hands that have painted many versions of this decoration over a lifetime.

* Delft was developed by potters during the earlier part of the seventeenth century to mimic the coveted blue and white Ming porcelains imported from China by the Dutch East India Company. The copying was so successful that from a distance it's hard to tell the difference between the two. On closer inspection however, one can see that the Chinese porcelain is translucent and fine compared to the thicker, heavier earthenware delft. When porcelain was discovered in Europe in the mid-eighteenth century, the popularity of the delft dwindled, however delft continues to be made even today.

Scalloped bowl

This rooster is a small motif in the centre of a scalloped serving bowl that hangs to the left of my parents' stove. It has hung in my parents' kitchen for as long as I can remember. I always thought the rooster looked a bit angry, but he is a fancy rooster as well. I love that he is standing on the fence — clearly in mid-crow. It embodies a sort of farm life that we actually lived. It is Portuguese, I believe, with a tin glaze and hand-painted. The colour palette influenced how my mother uses colour in her kitchen — especially the yellows, my mother has always liked a yellow kitchen. We never actually used this growing up, it has always hung as a decoration on the wall. I find that kind of remarkable.

* The rooster in Portuguese often refers to the legend of the Rooster of Barcelos.

A rich landowner in Barcelos held a banquet, during which a valuable piece of silver was stolen and a guest accused of the theft. The guest was tried by the court and found guilty. Despite the evidence against him, the guest protested his innocence and he was granted one final chance to prove it. Seeing a dead rooster nearby he said, 'If I am innocent, the cock will crow.' The cock crowed and the guest was allowed to go free.

There are many variations of the legend, but all include a plot that includes a dead rooster that crows, proving a man's innocence and therefore setting him free.

Dessert plate

This plate is small, about fifteen centimetres (six inches) in diameter. It matches a set of French covered bowls that I believe are actually for coffee or café au lait, but my mother has always used them as dessert dishes for puddings. Made with red earthenware clay, they are decorated with a white tin glaze and hand-painted with cobalt blue, yellow, green and pink brushwork, and I believe the pattern is from Brittany.

The dessert plates have many chips in them from use over the years, but they rarely came out when I was growing up. I remember having to get onto a chair to reach them from the cabinet, and the ceremonial feeling of pulling out the good china for a special occasion. In our home, we grew much of the food we ate and there was a particularly celebratory feeling about a special occasion or holiday meal — we were proud of the food we had grown and it tasted that much better for us having worked so hard to grow it. Meals were often big and a central part of our day.

*The French and English often refer to tin-glazed pottery as 'faience', although the term was originally a reference to the Italian tin-glazed wares imported to France from Faenza, Italy. Like delft, faience was a technique developed to mimic the desirable porcelains imported from the East. In France, faience manufacturing developed first in Brittany, in a factory near Quimper in the late seventeenth century.

Dinner plate

The circle is a close-up of a gold monogram on a set of Royal Crown Derby china that my mother inherited from her mother. The monogram is double crossed 'C's for Camilla — a name that goes back about eight generations on my mother's side of the family. As far as we know, my family set came directly from France. My mother told me the monogram was Catherine de' Medici's, and my ancestor had adopted it as her own. My mother loved this set — in its full glory, a table set with these simply decorated gold-rimmed plates and bowls were incredibly elegant and caught candlelight spectacularly. We even set out the little bread plates when we were celebrating an occasion and using this service. I was always in awe of the real gold and the shocking white of the porcelain; the bowls were wide and flat and clearly for fancy people.

When my parents sold the farm, when I was thirteen, my mother carefully packed all the dinner plates into a five-gallon plastic bucket. She was being very careful to store these precious plates and she put them in a shed next to our new house. Over that first winter, the shed roof leaked and the rain filled the bucket. When the winter came, the water froze around the plates and all of them cracked beyond repair. My mother was devastated. She still has the dessert plates, bread plates and soup bowls.

DERBY
5-05

By the late nineteenth century, it was very common for the wedding china of the daughter of a wealthy family in a cosmopolitan city to be hand-painted and monogrammed. French Limoges porcelain would have been a particularly fashionable order from a fancy city shop, or even ordered in person during travels abroad. Catherine de' Medici was the wife of King Henry II, and Queen of France from 1547 until her husband died in 1559. Her double C monogram was from between 1536 and 1547, when she was the Dauphine of France. A hairpin was recently discovered by archaeologists in a communal toilet at Fontainbleau Palace, and was identified as Catherine's thanks to the monogram at the top. It is a bit of a mystery as to how the hairpin ended up in a communal latrine that Catherine no doubt would not have used.

Platter

This floral motif sits very small in the centre of a thirty-five-centimetre (fourteen-inch) platter that my mother has in her cabinet. It is used decoratively, rarely with anything served on it. It is thick and somewhat unwieldy. It is made from red earthenware and has a white crackled tin glaze on the surface that makes me think it is an antique, but I am not sure that it actually is. The rim of the platter is scalloped with a trim pattern on it. It is definitely hand-painted. One way I can tell is the quirky nature of the hand — no two leaves are alike. The basket looks very similar to a common delft pattern, but with the way it is decorated and with no marking on the back, it is most likely a fake delft piece.

*There are a few ways to tell if you have a piece of authentic delftware. If the price is on the higher side, it is more likely actually hand-painted. But transfers are often well done, so it is hard to tell the difference. If you look at the base of the pot, take caution if you see 'Delft Blue' or 'hand-painted' written there. Sometimes these small details are actually painted over a transfer image to give it a more authentic look. Delftware from the nineteenth century onward usually has a trademark, and often the painter will initial a pot, or there is even a factory code on the base.

Pitcher

This is a very small jug: it only stands
about thirteen centimetres (five inches)
tall, and says it is a half-litre —
maybe close, but not exact. It is clearly
handmade, which makes me think it
is historic. It is a common Italian form,
possibly used for decanting and serving
wine. My mother always uses this
for small cut flowers from her garden.
It often sits on the kitchen table. One
of my favourite aspects of this jug
is the combination of fancy lettering
and motif on the surface of a pot.

Dinner plate

This Shenango blue willow plate was manufactured in the 1920s in Pennsylvania. It was gifted to my parents by my paternal grandparents, as part of a full set of dinner plates shortly after my parents were married in the late 1970s. Growing up, these plates were what my family ate off at most meals. I loved eating off the blue and white pattern — my mind would usually wander, speculating about the story that is illustrated in the surface decoration. Who is that man in the little boat? Why are those people crossing the bridge? What are they holding?

My brother and I favoured one of our blue willow plates that had been poorly made. It sat in a way that made the plate spin. This might have been an imperfection in the eyes of the adults at the table, but to my brother and me this made dinner into a game. We would argue over which of us got the 'spinny plate' and a rule that we had to take turns with it every other night was implemented. Our arguments got so common that my mother finally taped a quarter to the bottom of one of the other plates so that it would also spin. As a result, we could both spin our dinners to our heart's content and my parents could finally eat in peace, sort of. I remember seeking out the 'real spinny plate' over the imposter when it was my night to set the table.

The blue willow pattern is often associated with Chinese export blue and white porcelain, yet it was actually of European design. The first blue willow pattern was engraved by Thomas Minton and introduced to the market by Thomas Turner in 1780. Much of the most common contemporary blue willow china is actually transferware – not hand-painted. My family's blue willow plates are transferware made by Shenango domestically in the US. Shenango was the largest manufacturer of vitrified china in the world by the 1940s, manufacturing china for the US armed forces and even for the White House, including a commemorative plate for Dwight D. Eisenhower and dinnerware for Lyndon B. Johnson.

*See page 96/97 for the Blue Willow Story

Staffordshire spill vases

This is a pair of Staffordshire figurines that my grandmother Myma kept on the mantel in her living room. I remember being told not to touch them as a child, but desperately wanting to. How could you not want to touch these? Those little flowers behind each deer are delightful! They acted to frame the other objects on the mantel, giving edges and grounding the styling. Like a lot of the objects in my grandmother's home, these are small and intimate. They have been chipped and broken, mended and touched up with a little paint to make them look new — a common repair in my grandmother's home. They now sit on a chest in my parents' living room doing a similar job of framing the items on the chest as on my grandmother's mantel above her fireplace.

CROWN
STAFFORDSHIRE
ENGLAND
A.D.1801.

* The figurines were originally part of a larger object called a spill vase, made by Staffordshire around 1820. It makes sense that my grandmother had them on her mantelpiece and then in her dining room sideboard because a spill vase is a small cylinder vase that is meant to hold rolled paper or thin sticks called spills, and tapers. You would light the spills in the fireplace and transfer the flame to a candle, a lamp or use it to light tobacco.

Mugs

When Myma wasn't painting in her studio, she was often sitting at her kitchen table with a cup of coffee and a cigarette. Many of my fondest memories are of sitting with her and listening to stories from her life. These four mugs are from Win Ng Animates series from the late 1970s.

I remember all of these designs, perhaps from her kitchen, perhaps not. I particularly remember her having the cat, or one similar. The hue of the cobalt blue is very strong and looks less commercial than most manufactured mugs from that time. I loved the use of humorous subject matter with text and image as well as the blue and white colour palette.

* Win Ng was a mid-century artist from the San Francisco Bay area. He was influential in the art scene in the 1950s and made a name for himself as a ceramic artist, initially as a sculptor and then later in his career Ng shifted his focus to functional ceramics. He teamed up with Spaulding Taylor to co-found Taylor and Ng. which grew to a large company with many employees. Ng is well known for his ability to work well in both the worlds of fine arts and commercial arts. While the department store Taylor and Ng closed in 1985, there is an online retailer of the same name that has reissued many of the original designs.

Molly Hatch   A Passion for China

Tobacco jar

This is the motif on the exterior of
a very large, fifty-one centimeters
(twenty-inch) French tobacco jar.
The tin glaze has this hand-painted
design with lettering on the front and
back — both sides decorated the same
way. Tobacco jars were a large part
of proper storage of tobacco imported
to Europe from the US. The tobacco
jar had a prominent place in the home.
Most are ceramics, earthenware in
particular, and they typically have a lid
with a hole for a damp sponge helping
to keep the tobacco moist. There were
a pair of these in my grandmother's
kitchen that were made into lamps.

My family were ship builders in
Maine at one point, and they imported
china as ballast in the ships —
including, the story goes, this jar.
This example of a ceramic surface
decorated with text and image
has influenced my own designs.

Tabac

Delft figurines

These ceramic lions, according to family lore, are said to be Roman, though my Uncle Josh (who now has these) and I both agree this is probably not the case. Early eighteenth-century Dutch delft is more likely. They are small, sixteen centimeters (six inches) tall. They sat in front of a huge silver mirror on a side table in my grandmother's kitchen.

They have been badly broken and repaired multiple times with the signature paint touch-up to make them look more whole again, and in this case they have been touched up in the back of the piece, not visible from the most important view – the front. They sat on the table well within reach of small hands, and with close to thirty grandchildren and seven of her own children, it's no surprise these were broken and repaired. They have these holes for ears and incredibly expressive eyes that are fabulous. I love the detail of the hair and mane, the black graphic outlines are wonderful and weird.

* These lions are very similar to others
I have found from the Netherlands.
I have even found some comparable lion
figures that were made in Brussels in
the eighteenth century. But most likely
these are Dutch delft models of a Dutch
Republic Lion, coming before the
current coat of arms of the kingdom
of the Netherlands.

Mugs

My mother is a coffee drinker, and a tea drinker. There is a running joke about the kettle being on wherever my mother is in the house, because she always has a cup of something in hand. My mother has this little quirk where she licks the side of the cup after she sips to catch the little drip down the side.

Growing up we had a lot of different mugs to choose from — always mugs, rarely teacups. This one is decorated with a copper wash on a tin white glaze over red earthenware clay. It is soft in many ways — the colour bleeds into the glaze, the walls are thick and cosy, and even the handle is round and fat. When I look at this mug, I think of my mother sipping coffee in her window seat in the living room as she writes in her daily journal.

Another of my favourite mugs from my parents' home. This is hand-painted and sort of a silly rooster. It is a cheery mug that sits well with the colours my mother loves in her kitchen. We always had chickens growing up. I remember having a couple roosters as well, they were typically short-lived. There was one rooster in particular who had a habit of waking our family with his cock-a-doodle-doo around 3 a.m. every night. He lived an especially short life, if you know what I mean ...

*
Mini history
of the teacup and
mug overleaf

THE HISTORY OF THE TEACUP

The evolution of the teacup began in China and spread through Europe in the seventeenth century as a handle-free vessel. There is no Latin word for tea because tea didn't travel the silk roads all the way to the West. Tea only made it to Europe in about 1600, with the Dutch and the Portuguese carrying it home in ships along with the other oriental trade. Chinese teacups had no handles and were held by the thumb and forefinger at the lip and base of the cup. At first they brewed their tea in the same cups they drank from.

Later they invented teapots, using a durable 'hard-clay' — a material strong enough to withstand scalding heat. But while these teapots had handles, the cups did not.

In their early days of tea drinking, Europeans poured their tea into saucers to cool before sipping; this was perfectly acceptable. This is what writers of the period mean by 'a dish of tea'. As the popularity of tea spread, craftsmen and hostesses alike struggled with ways to improve tea service. Although silver was a durable metal, it transferred heat too well. Over the course of the seventeenth century, the transition from fine silver cups to porcelain ones began. European factories Meissen and Sèvres started making their own porcelain after the Chinese model — pretty cups, with and without handles, and equally pretty bowl-like saucers for them. By the mid- to late eighteenth century, tea officially graduated to a cup with a handle and drinking tea from a 'dish' became old-fashioned.

In 1657 Thomas Garway started serving tea in his London coffee house to 'Persons of Quality' and by 1700 there were approximately 500 coffee houses serving tea. The British government tried to take advantage of tea's popularity by taxing tea, and requiring coffee houses to have a license to serve tea. Increasing taxes resulted in the common practice of tea smuggling. And since tea was in such high demand, tea smugglers often tried to sneak in fillers from other plants.

Tea was first brought to North America by the Dutch, also in the seventeenth century. The Dutch colony of New Amsterdam was acquired by the English, who renamed the settlement New York and passed on many of the tea drinking customs that were common in England. The tea trade between the English colonies and England were centred in these major cities during the 1720s. Tea was heavily taxed and tea smuggling was as prevalent as it was in England, due to the East India Company's monopoly on tea imports. One tax in particular, the tea tax passed by an Act of Parliament in 1767, caused even more dissent and rebellion among the American colonists, leading to the famous Boston Tea Party rebellion.

Jar

This little landscape is from a nineteenth-century French powder puff jar. This set was given to my grandmother Myma by her French relative when she was a little girl. Myma admired it so much that her relative gifted it to her right off her dressing table. My grandmother kept it on her dressing table and when my mother was admiring it one day, my grandmother gave it to her. And, as you can imagine, I was gifted this off my mother's dresser when I admired it as a child. It is delicate, and perhaps the only pink thing I have ever known my mother to have in her possession.

Dinner plate

My family always had Thanksgiving with my father's parents, Grammie Dot and Grampa Jim. Thanksgiving dinner always began with a strange cranberry Jell-O salad with grapes and cranberries and walnuts, served over an iceberg lettuce wedge with a dollop of miracle whip as dressing (which I LOVED, by the way). We always had turkey with trimmings, of course. This Currier and Ives pattern was my grandparents' everyday china.

The Ohio-based Royal China Company started production of this line of Currier and Ives china in 1950, and it was available in several colours: blue, brown and red. The scenes of Americana were a huge success with the growing American middle class, whose taste had recently turned to a revival of Early American Bicentennial decor around this time. The tableware was sold widely in department stores and even given as premiums by the A&P grocery chain — there was an A&P in Woodstock, Vermont where my grandparents lived out the majority of their lives. Part of me wonders if they acquired their set via A&P.

My grandparents were both born and raised in New England and the snowy landscape on these plates seems to describe their childhoods to me. Whenever I see this tableware pattern, my thoughts immediately go to Thanksgiving dinner at Grammie and Grandpa's.

* Currier and Ives tableware was produced for thirty-six years with only a brief interruption from 1970-5. The patterns were discontinued in 1986.

Plate

My mother inherited this set of German Dresden china from her father. We stored it away in a cabinet for the most part, but on special occasions we would pull this service out, along with some of the others you have already been introduced to. I adored this service as a little girl. Between the gold detailing and the different arrangement of flowers on each plate it was feminine and decorative in an indulgent sort of way. I always had a hard time choosing which plate would be mine as I set the table. The paintings on these plates are delicate and detailed, most certainly painted with a teeny, tiny brush. My own hand isn't capable of being so fine.

*The mark on the base of these plates is that of German Dresden porcelain, however Dresden porcelain has often been confused with German Meissen porcelain. This may be because Dresden in Germany is the home to both the Meissen and Dresden factories. The first porcelain factory in Europe was set up just outside the city after the secret to hard-paste porcelain production was first discovered under the reign of Augustus the Strong, but the wares were actually sold in Dresden. The result was that Meissen figurines were commonly referred to as Dresden porcelain even though they were marked with the Meissen crossed swords. Dresden porcelain is characterized by the use of flowers, fruits, shells, foliage and scrolls, and was popularized during the nineteenth century.

Jar

Myrna had this fabulous hexagonal lamp
in her living room — a lamp that used
to be a jar of some kind, repurposed. This
image is one panel of the lamp — each
side has some sort of saint illustrated
on it. I love the little details of the sun
poking out from the sky and the face of
a cherub looking down. I have no idea
who the saints are, but the lamp seems
old. Decorated with brushwork over
a white tin glaze, it looks like it could be
eighteenth-century, maybe even earlier.

S. SEBASTIANUS

Gravy boat

This is a Fitzhugh china gravy boat. My mother inherited this recently from my Aunt Kaela (my mother's eldest sister). Apparently this is one piece of a full service that my grandmother Myma had inherited, which had originally been imported as ballast in ships.

My mother married a farmer and was very much living a farmer's life when my grandmother decided it was time to pass on the Fitzhugh china to her children. However, when my mother exclaimed how good my grandmother's timing was because she couldn't afford to buy plates, my grandmother took offence at the intention of using the china on a daily basis and decided against giving any of the service to my mother. Years later, after my grandmother passed away, my aunt found out about my mother not receiving any of the Fitzhugh china and gifted my mother this single gravy boat, without its saucer. It is the only piece of Fitzhugh we have.

Turns out, my grandmother was probably right about the value of the china and it being only for truly special occasions. I looked up the going rate for this gravy boat in the secondary and antiques market, and in good condition, with its saucer, it is worth a significant amount.

* Fitzhugh porcelain was a Chinese export porcelain and commonly brought to the US as ballast in ships from 1775-1850. It continues to be one of the more highly valued Chinese export porcelains on the antique market today. The pattern can be recognized by the border with central medallion with four panels of decorations surrounding it.

Plate

This plate is a fantastic example of the colour palette in Myma's home. My grandmother bought a set of these plates when visiting Normandy, France with her second husband, Creighton. Creighton was a wine reviewer, and they travelled in France and Europe occasionally for his work. These are beautiful examples of French faience pottery, which is tin glaze over red clay with hand-painted decoration. The dark blue with the crest in the centre and all of the floral detailing is classic, and I see so much of my own aesthetic mirrored in these plates. I had forgotten about them until working on this project, when my Aunt Tisha sent me some photos. I remember them now, and everything about them speaks of Myma and especially the colours of her home.

*On the back of this plate it is signed 'St. Pierre-en-Port' which is in the Normandy region of France. It is a farming village with pebble beaches and high limestone cliffs overlooking the English Channel. This area was very touristic in the early twentieth century, but was hit hard during the Second World War.

MVSEVM OF FINE ARTS

Chapter 2

What I Learned at the Museum

THE STORY OF
HOW PORCELAIN CAME
TO THE WEST

The history of ceramics stretches back thousands of years. Ceramic as a material is fragile but largely doesn't change over time: a plate painted a few hundred years ago will retain the vibrancy and sharpness of colour that it had the day it was removed from the kiln. There is something particularly comforting about knowing that the ceramic objects we visit in a museum are as they have always been. This 'sameness' provides a sort of connectivity to the past.

As a student at the School of the Museum of Fine Arts, I had unlimited admission to most of the museums in Boston and I regularly took advantage of this perk. I often found respite in the Museum of Fine Arts. The quiet of the galleries and the vastness of the space helped me adjust from my country childhood to my new city life as a college student.

Being able to visit the museum and see in person many of the objects and paintings I was studying in my art history courses added a depth of understanding I am not sure I would have gotten otherwise. The study of museum collections has become a large part of my working process as an artist.

Museum of Fine Arts, Boston

A year after graduating from university, I travelled around Europe with the main objective of seeing as many of the famous European museums and their collections as I could in six months. I fell in love with the Victoria and Albert Museum in London. I felt like I had stumbled on a sort of shrine to the objects we live with. Gallery after gallery held objects I had coveted in books — wallpaper I lusted after, ceramic objects made by my pottery heroes ... I was so engrossed by what I was seeing there that I didn't bring out my camera once to document what I was experiencing.

More recently, my travels brought me to Paris where the Musée des Arts Décoratifs had finally reopened (on my first trip to Europe it was closed for renovations), and it has become an addition to my ever-growing list of favourite museums.

In addition to my time as a student at the Museum of Fine Arts in Boston, I now live quite close to New York City and regularly frequent the collections at the Metropolitan Museum of Art.

All of these museum collections have greatly informed my research for this chapter. There is a subtle kind of study that happens when you visit a museum over and over, and you repeatedly visit favourite objects. It feels like visiting old friends every time you go, and each time the objects reveal something new that you hadn't noticed before. Here on these pages, the old friends that I visit whenever I can in Boston, New York, London and Paris help to illustrate the travel of porcelain from the East to the West, and the passion for porcelain that was ignited as a result.

View from the top floor of the Musée des Arts Décoratifs, September, 2015

A QUICK DEFINITION OF PORCELAIN

Porcelain is a ceramic material that is made up largely of kaolin. Kaolin is a soft white clay that is the natural result of decomposing feldspar. Porcelain is one of the most vitreous (glass-like) clays when fired in a kiln to its maturity — usually at temperatures between 1,200°C and 1,400°C (2,200°F and 2,600°F). Because porcelain is so vitreous, it is well known for its durability.

The English word porcelain derives from the Italian word *porcellana*, which roughly translates to 'cowrie shell' in English. It may be that the explorer Marco Polo was one of the first to use the term *porcellana* to describe the material he saw on his travels in China, as the translucence of porcelain is similar to the translucence of the cowrie shell.

Porcelain is commonly called china in English-speaking countries and this is likely because the country China was the original source.

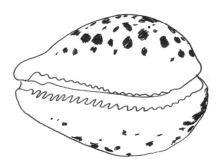

FROM ASIA TO THE MIDDLE EAST

My research at the Museum of Fine Arts in Boston, to find some of my old favourite pots to help illustrate this chapter, was rewarding and sentimental. The Museum of Fine Arts is vast — remodelled since my last visit, its architecture matches the grandeur of its contents. Despite the remodel, the hallways that led me to the Asian and Middle Eastern ceramics collections were largely unchanged. There is something satisfying and even comforting knowing that, as my life has propelled forward since being a student, my old friends have held court in the same spot the entire time. I quickly found my way back to the familiar vitrines, knowing which pieces I wanted to record and gather to bring home, not really expecting to discover some new things along my way. But the *sancai* covered jar (see page 68) and the Song Dynasty porcelain carved plate (see page 72) were both new discoveries for me, unearthed during my recent research for this book.

Metropolitan Museum of Art, New York

Molly Hatch   A Passion for China

A QUICK HISTORY OF PORCELAIN

The earliest porcelain wares are said to date as far back as 100–200 BC, China. It was during the Tang Dynasty (AD 618–907) that porcelain began to be regularly exported to the Islamic world, starting a long history of the Chinese export of porcelain.

Some of the first export wares are known for their tri-colour glazed surfaces, also called *sancai* wares. Skills were perfected and production levels of porcelain had to keep up with unprecedented demand from the export trade in the Song Dynasty (960–1279). It was during the Ming Dynasty (1368–1644) that the most porcelain was being exported to Europe. During this time, export trade routes from China to the West were expanded from the Middle East, following the Silk Road to Europe. Portuguese merchants were the first to trade with China by sea, starting in the fifteenth century, and in the early seventeenth century Dutch merchants also began trading extensively with China by sea, bringing even more export porcelain to Europe.

| 28,000BC | | Han Dynasty 206BC–220AD | Tang Dynasty 618–907 | Song Dynasty 960–1279 |

28,000BC
'Věstonická Venuše', a 30,000-year-old ceramic figure from Dolní Věstonice, Czech Republic, which is believed to be the oldest ceramic figure in the world.

24,000BC
Ceramic art in China is the longest, continuously evolving art form, which dates all the way back to 24,000BC. Ceramic figurines used for ceremonial purposes.

206BC–220AD
Porcelain invented in China.

600
Porcelain exported from China to some Muslim countries via Silk Road.

1271
Marco Polo's first trip to Asia.

Marco Polo

| | | Qing Dynasty 1644–1912 | | |

1602
Dutch East India Company established.

Dutch capture Portuguese cargo ships bearing thousands of pieces of Ming porcelain.

1620
Dutch begin imitating Chinese porcelain.

1650
France: Chinese-style blue and white wares produced for the first time in France.

1693
France: first important French porcelain was made at the St Cloud factory.

1708
Germany: Tschirnhaus makes a hard, white, translucent type of porcelain.

Molly Hatch   A Passion for China

Yuan Dynasty
1279–1368

Ming Dynasty
1368–1664

1279–1368
Use of cobalt:
the cobalt the
Chinese potters
first encountered
in the late
Yuan to early
Ming period
(14th century)
was imported
from the
Near East.

1338
Fonthill Vase
arrives in Europe.

1492
Christopher
Columbus sets
sail from Spain
with the *Niña*,
Pinta and
Santa Maria.

1513
First Portuguese
ship arrives
in China.

1575
Beginning of
Medici porcelain.

1710
Germany:
Meissen Factory
opens.

1712
France:
Jesuit father
Francois Xavier
d'Entrecolles
letters reveal
China's porcelain
methodology.

1743
England:
Bow claims to
produce first
English hard-
paste porcelain.

1745
England:
Chelsea factory
produces hard-
paste porcelain.

1751
England:
Worcester Tonquin
Manufacture
factory founded
where 70% of its
total output is blue
and white ware.

Covered jar

I particularly love how the glaze moves over the surface of this pot — clearly intentional; the potter here worked hard to allow glaze to do what it does best: melt. The amber-coloured glaze moves the most over the surface, causing a typical pattern of this style to form over the pot as the glaze melted in the heat of the kiln. The potter's addition of a line of texture drawn into the surface of the lid and at the top of the belly of the jar encourages the glaze to pool, showing off and taking advantage of how it moves as it melts. Also, at the bottom where the glaze meets the clay, there are visible drips where the glaze almost reaches the bottom of the pot. The maker knew that this would happen, so there is a large area of unglazed clay, which allows for the glaze to melt and move down the pot, but not actually move off the pot.

* This pot is a great example of the tri-colour ware of the Chinese Tang Dynasty that was so sought after in the Islamic region. This piece is not porcelain, however it is a very good example of the typical coloration of the 'sancai' wares.

China, Tang dynasty, AD 618– 907.
Decorated with tri-colour (sancai) glaze

Bowl

The shape of this bowl is inherited from the white Chinese porcelains of the Tang Dynasty that were so admired in Iraq, but the lustre decoration is typical of Islam. This bowl is a good example of how Chinese export porcelains were influencing the Islamic potters who worked hard to mimic the look of porcelain by using white glazes over their local dark-coloured clay. My interest in this pot is the repetitive mark making that was used to shade the area behind the warrior, as well as the softness of the lustre surface that is in contrast to the subject of the imagery. It is hard to imagine making this kind of bowl without today's technology. It is clean of any imperfections or speckles of iron in the surface; at the time this would have been achieved with skill and attention to detail.

*Lustre firing was one of Islam's great contributions to ceramic history. To add lustre to the bowl, the potter painted this glazed bowl with metal oxides, and fired it again, finishing the surface of the glaze with a thin layer of shiny metal with the effect of gold. The materials and double firing made this technique expensive to perform, making this pot likely to have been made for the court. Lustreware is often decorated with designs associated with the court, such as this warrior who holds a flag and a sword.

Iraq, tenth century. Earthenware
painted in lustre on an opaque
white glaze

Dish with floral design

The delicate carving in the surface of this dish, with its simple white coloration, is in line with Taoism and neo-Confucianism, the popular Chinese philosophies of this time. The carving takes advantage of what porcelain does best. Porcelain's hard vitreous surface can hold an incredible level of detail, unlike many other clays which tend to crumble when carved. The use of a simple glaze that pools slightly into the carved areas is stunning and draws the viewer in closely. A subtle and graceful accentuation of the carving happens as a result of the perfect porcelain and glaze combination.

*This dish would have been fired in a kiln fuelled by wood. Burning wood creates lots of ash that contaminates the glaze on the surface of a pot. This means that this pot would have been fired inside two pots, acting like a box surrounding the dish. This box is called a 'saggar' and acts to keep the surface of the porcelain clean and free from imperfections.

China, Northern Song-Jin Dynasty,
twelfth-century Ding ware.
Porcellaneous stoneware, with
incised design

Dish in Chinese style

My love of blue and white wares was clearly fostered in my childhood — and I love a good floral. The complexity and mathematical symmetry of this pot inspired many hours of study. I wondered how the maker figured out how to make the pattern repeat work just right on the surface of the piece, knowing well that one smudge with the cobalt pigment could ruin the whole pot. In my own work I aimed to make brushstrokes look as effortless as these, but it took many years to realize that only with a deep knowledge of the process and material (and possibly 10,000 hours of practice) might I come closer to achieving a similar look in my own ceramic surfaces.

*During the fifteenth and sixteenth centuries, blue and white porcelain wares from China were admired and collected in the courts of Iran and Turkey. Although potters of these areas lacked the raw materials for making porcelain, they worked to imitate the colour scheme and designs of the expensive imports. Some of their wares copy Chinese originals entirely, but more often they combine Chinese-inspired motifs with the local motifs and patterning.

North-west Iran, c. 1500. Stonepaste
body, cobalt blue painted on white
slip underglaze

Large bowl with blue and white decoration of landscape

This bowl is typical of the export wares we in the West are more familiar with, from the Ming Dynasty in China. This decoration of a landscape in blue and white is the kind of imagery often emulated in European faience and early European porcelains. In the seventeenth and eighteenth centuries,

Chinese blue and white porcelain was highly prized in Europe because a European source for kaolin (the main ingredient in porcelain) was yet to be found. Porcelain was collected by European aristocracy. Considered even more valuable than gold, it was sometimes referred to as 'white gold'.

China, late Ming dynasty. Early
seventeenth-century Porcelain,
Dehua ware painted in underglaze blue

A MINI HISTORY OF COBALT BLUE IN CHINA

In the early fourteenth century, mass production of fine, translucent, blue and white porcelain started in Jingdezhen, a city often referred to as the porcelain capital of China.

The development of blue and white surface decoration was due to the combination of Chinese techniques and cobalt from Persia brought home by Chinese traders along trade routes with Islam. Cobalt blue pigment was considered a precious commodity, with a value about twice that of gold at this time. The cobalt imported to China was mixed with an arsenic contaminant that made the blues brighter and more intense. Many early

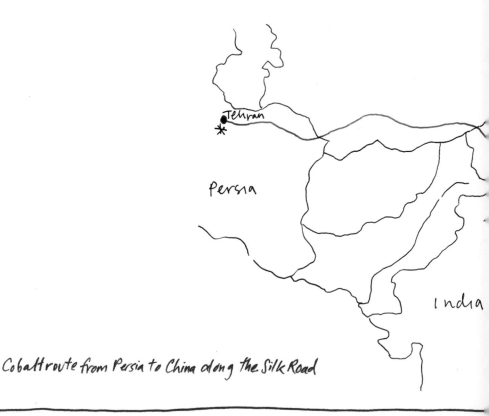

Cobalt route from Persia to China along the Silk Road

Chinese motifs in blue and white porcelains are inspired by Islamic surface decorations.

From the late fifteenth or early sixteenth century, local Chinese sources of cobalt blue were discovered, but the Chinese cobalt had manganese impurities mixed in, somewhat dulling the blues and making them softer and less intense. As a result, Persian cobalt remained the most sought after and therefore the most expensive. During the seventeenth century, Chinese potters began to mix the imported cobalt and the local cobalt to create an altogether new cobalt blue. Production of blue and white wares continues in Jingdezhen to this day.

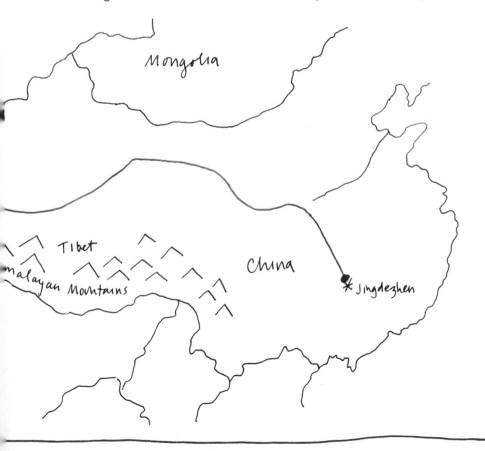

HOW PORCELAIN WAS DISCOVERED IN EUROPE

My first visit to the Musée des Arts Décoratifs in Paris was only last year. Walking into the long central hall on the first floor of the museum felt like entering a decorative arts sanctuary. I had found my decorative art 'home away from home' in Paris. The permanent eighteenth-century decorative arts installation perhaps reminded me of first falling in love with porcelain — with room after room of beautiful objects from Sèvres, Vincennes and other French porcelain manufacturers. The museum was digestible in scale and reminiscent of the palace in which it resides.

Chinese export porcelain was so valued in eighteenth-century Europe that the common English use of the term china replaced the term porcelain, and the popularity led to many European attempts to replicate it. But the Chinese techniques and formula for the composition were a well-guarded secret. The development of soft-paste Medici porcelain in sixteenth-century Florence was Europe's first attempt at making porcelain with some success. It looked similar and worked similarly, but just wasn't quite the same quality as the Chinese.

Early on in merchant trading with China, also in the sixteenth century, the Portuguese brought home samples of raw unfired kaolin, which they understood to be the essential ingredient in the production of porcelain. But all attempts resulted in unpredictable outcomes and failure.

Then in 1708 Ehrenfried Walther von Tschirnhaus and Johann Friedrich Böttger made the first true sample of a vitreous white, translucent type of porcelain. They did this with a combination of ingredients, including the first kaolin found in Europe, from a mine in Colditz which Germany kept secret. The Meissen factory was established in 1710 after the development of a kiln and a glaze suitable for use with the porcelain.

Then, in 1712, Chinese porcelain manufacturing secrets were revealed to the French Jesuit father Francois Xavier d'Entrecolles. He published them in a series of letters called the *Lettres édifiantes et curieuses de Chine par des missionnaires jésuites.*

Musée des Arts Décoratifs, Paris

Chocolate pot and cover

The use of colour in the surface of this pot is exciting (and a little over the top), not only because it is something other than blue and white, but also in its use of so many colours. The application of this colour as an enamel in additional firings would have significantly increased the cost to make the work, not to mention the formulating needed to have all of these colours on hand.

It is the skill of the painting in much of Meissen porcelain that I am drawn to. Imagine a time when porcelain was worth the same amount as gold — could you imagine painting on top of a pot made of gold? I think it is hard for us to imagine the value of these objects when they were made because we do not value porcelain the same way today.

*Tschirnhaus was already part of the European search for porcelain when Johann Böttger was appointed to assist him in 1705. They were both employed by the King of Poland, Augustus II the Strong, and worked in Dresden. Böttger had originally trained as a pharmacist and later as an alchemist; he claimed to know the secret of changing dross into gold, which, of course, attracted the attention of Augustus II the Strong, who imprisoned him until he could prove this ability. As a result of many years of failure, Böttger was eventually assigned to work for Tschirnhaus, leading to the discovery of the first formula for porcelain in Europe.

Meissen, Germany, c 1740. Decorated
Netherlands, c 1750. Hard-paste
porcelain, enamelled and gilded to
replicate Chinese famille-rose

THE FONTHILL VASE
NATIONAL MUSEUM OF IRELAND

The Fonthill Vase (aka Gaignières-Fonthill Vase) is a blueish-white Chinese porcelain vase dated to AD 1300–40. It is the earliest documented Chinese porcelain object to have reached Europe.

Whilst looking at this vase, I thought a lot about the story of its travels and that it is likely the object that initially spurred on our cultural love and obsession with porcelain in the West. The vase was made in Jingdezhen, China and was first part of a collection of Louis the Great of Hungary, who seems to have received it from a Chinese ambassador as a gift.

The vase was mounted with a silver handle and base, transforming it into a ewer and gifted to Charles III of Naples in 1381. As I painted, I also found myself wondering how this vase actually came into the hands of that Chinese ambassador? It likely came across Islam and through eastern Europe on horseback. Packed in what kind of material? It's amazing to think of a piece this fragile making it all the way on the back of an animal!

The vase was then gifted out of Naples to the duc de Barry and moved on again to be gifted to the dauphin of France, living in the

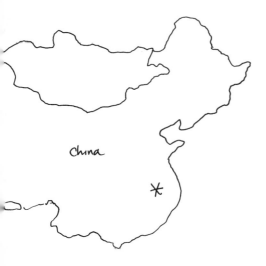

China

*

halls of Versailles. There is some thought that a collector had it until the French Revolution, when Englishman William Beckford acquired the vase at an auction.

Beckford kept the vase in his palace at Fonthill (hence the name) and it resurfaced in 1882 at a sale by Beckford's heirs at Hamilton Palace without its silver mounts. The vase was then lost to public view until it was rediscovered in the 1950s and acquired for a small sum. It is now in the National Museum of Ireland.

While tracking the travels of the Fonthill Vase is interesting in itself, I find it particularly hard to imagine that *this* vase is what spearheaded the mountains of porcelain exported from the East to the West. The vase itself is not the finest example of what potters were capable of at this time. Don't get me wrong, it is still lovely, but the flowers, which are a dimensional applied aspect aren't very refined and the strings of a sort of beaded texture seem to trail off with unintentional endings; the overall attention to detail in this piece seems lacking. I love that there was a point in the history of this object where it was transformed into a ewer with an added handle and spout. I have pondered how it was meant to function, but realize that it likely was never meant to actually function as a ewer, but as an exotic and valuable decorative object.

Ewer

This ewer form is such a marriage of Italianate decorative elements — the handles and the spout in particular feel Italian to me, while the shape of the body of the ewer seems to be pulled directly from Chinese history. I really enjoy seeing this merging of aesthetic — like a version of the children's game of Chinese whispers, when a message changes through interpretation as it moves down the line of people. There is a lovely richness to seeing one culture interpret another, take what they are attracted to and leave behind what they are not.

✗Medici porcelain was the first identifiable porcelain produced in Europe to imitate Chinese porcelain. The manufactory in Florence existed between 1575 and 1587 under the patronage of Francesco I de' Medici, Grand Duke of Tuscany, to make porcelain imitations of Chinese blue and white wares, which were so highly prized in Europe. Approximately sixty pieces of Medici porcelain are known to have survived. Hard-paste porcelain is fired at around 1,400°C, and is usually made of a compound of kaolin and petunse. In an effort to copy the Chinese hard-paste porcelain Europeans developed soft-paste porcelain, a white porcelain compound of kaolin and glass frit fired at lower temperatures, making it 'softer' and less durable (firing to temperatures around 1,200°C). Soft-paste porcelain is a less 'plastic' clay due to being mixed with frit and is therefore less suitable for potter's wheel and more suitable to carving.

Molly Hatch   A Passion for China

Medici, Florence, c. 1575-87,
Soft-paste porcelain

'Sample' plate

The yellow ground on this plate is striking to me because it is an unusual colour for delft — the blue and white is complemented by the yellow ground, making it visually pop. I am always drawn to ceramic wares that depict other ceramics on them. I love the thought that this plate may have been an early marketing tool for delft potters to display wares for sale. An early sort of product catalogue. I can picture an eighteenth-century Dutch travelling salesman pulling out his sample plate to show his potential customer what the factory can do. The little windows depicting scenes are fantastic in their goofy narratives — I can't help but think that the little man on the bottom left will be holding that bird for eternity, or the man on the left side of the plate will be running in place forever …

*The Dutch were second to the Portuguese as major importers of Chinese porcelain to Europe in the seventeenth and eighteenth centuries. The Dutch passion for porcelain led to their domestic development of the tin-glazed delftware that mimicked the prized blue and white wares of China. This is one of a pair of eighteenth-century delft plates that was inspired by Chinese originals. Later in the century Dutch ceramics gradually became less dependent on Asian models of production and design, and more humorous designs were widely imitated and produced.

Molly Hatch   A Passion for China

The Netherlands, 1750-75,
Delft, tin-glazed

Vase

This pair of vases shows heavy inspiration from the Chinese both in their shape and their surface, and yet somehow they feel far more French to me than Chinese. There are little details that point me to this, like in the flowers in the necks of the vases that look almost as though they were collaged into the pattern. It is fun to catch these moments where a piece really becomes an outside interpretation of another culture — though here the mimicking of Chinese patterns and surfaces is actually a copy of Chinese export wares, and the Chinese who made the originals, made them for what they imagined the European market wanting, not what they themselves might value. So in the end, who knows what is truly 'Chinese' about these, most likely very little.

*It was at the Nevers factory that Chinese-style blue and white wares were produced for the first time in France, with production running between 1650 and 1680. Nevers was the first French factory to mimic Chinese decorative motifs in the surfaces of their wares (in the case of this pair of vases, faience - similar in technique to the Dutch delftwares) Interestingly, the Nevers factory added manganese purple to their cobalt, distinguishing the Nevers blue from other blue and white wares of the time.

Nevers, France, seventeenth-century Faience

Molly Hatch   A Passion for China

Vase

This vase plays to my love of the baroque with its scrolling foliage and garlands, and little bugs flying above the drapery. There is a delicate nature to the surface of this pot that I almost feel could only be French. This type of imagery always has me wondering about how it came about — it is nonsense — a sort of imaginary world where everything is floating or stacked impossibly. The creatures are non-existent yet somehow it all feels as though it references something.

*The first soft-paste porcelain in France was developed in an effort to imitate high-value Chinese porcelain and followed the attempts of Medici porcelain in the sixteenth century. The first was produced at the Rouen factory in 1673 and became known as 'Porcelaine française'. The soft-paste porcelain lacked the kaolin needed to make hard-paste porcelain. It wasn't until around 1710 that kaolin was finally discovered in France and the Rouen factory began to produce true porcelain.

Manufacture de Saint-Cloud, 1695–1700, Soft-paste porcelain

PORCELAIN COMES TO ENGLAND

My first trip to the V&A in London was mainly to see the William Morris work in their collections. Once inside, my love for the museum was instantaneous. How could I not fall in love with a museum that dedicated the top floor to ceramics? I walked through the grand halls, examining vitrine after vitrine full of pots by all of my ceramic heroes — British and otherwise — all waiting to be discovered. Seeing the collections there, looking at so many of the objects I had studied but never seen in person, gave me a sense of connection to the makers of the past in a way I had not yet experienced.

In England the search for domestic porcelain had a similar interest and fervour as on the continent — let's not forget that porcelain was worth more than gold at its peak — who wouldn't want to find the formula and manufacture it? But the British were far behind other Europeans, and were not able to develop a reliable formula for porcelain until the mid-to late eighteenth century.

It seems that there is an ongoing historic debate in England about which factory in England was actually the first to manufacture porcelain. Royal Worcester (established in 1751) is said to be the oldest or second oldest remaining English porcelain brand still in existence today (in competition with Royal Crown Derby, established in 1750). It appears that the Chelsea Porcelain Factory was established in 1743, with the Bow Porcelain Factory opening on its heels in 1747. Regardless of who came first, it's clear that England had discovered domestic porcelain by the mid-1700s.

Like the European porcelain factories, the British imitated Chinese blue and white wares in their own designs. Although the domestic market was full of British porcelain copies, the competition from Chinese imports was strong. The British invention of transfer printing for surface decoration allowed for a more mechanized and therefore cheaper process — China's extensive and economic production of porcelain meant that the hand-painted Chinese wares were still able to undersell the domestic porcelains. It was the imposition of 150 per cent duties by the British in 1790 that finally led to the commercial success of domestic porcelain wares in England.

Victoria and Albert Museum, London

THE BLUE WILLOW

On the right side of the pattern you see a stately Chinese home: this is the home of a mandarin. The mandarin's gardener, Chang, and the mandarin's daughter, Koong-see, fall in love with each other and meet clandestinely. The mandarin finds out and forbids them to see each other. He locks his daughter in the house and builds a high wooden fence to stop the lovers from meeting. The mandarin also promises his daughter in marriage to a wealthy viceroy, Ta-jin, as soon as the peach tree blossoms in spring.

Koong-see spends her time watching the tree with apprehension, and when blossoms begin to appear, Chang sends a message in a floating bottle on the water with a plan for them to escape together. Koong-see takes with her a box of jewels that are meant to be her dowry and she and Chang escape over the bridge where you see three figures — Koong-see and Chang chased by the mandarin. The house at the foot of the bridge represents the home where Chang and Koong-see take refuge, with the help of

former servants of the mandarin, and where they marry.

The newly wed couple travel upriver on a houseboat to a new home, where they farm the land and are happy for some time. The mandarin posts a reward for the return of his jewels and his daughter, and the lovers are discovered by soldiers. Escorted back to the mandarin's home, jewels returned, the lovers are sent to his dungeons where they are lost to the labyrinth of the tunnels below, represented in the geometry of the border of the plate.

The gods pity Koong-see and Chang's sacrifice to their love of each other and reincarnate them as a pair of immortal doves that fly together forever at the top of the pattern.

Basket

My interest in this basket is not just for its typical Chinese-style blue and white surface decoration but as a great example of what Worcester was well known for. It reminds me of a basket we had on a side table in our family farmhouse kitchen growing up. My mother kept fruit in the basket — which we were allowed to snack on any time. I remember carefully choosing an apple from the basket and admiring the ceramic florets and cut-out sections making it look truly like a basket, only made of porcelain.

*According to the Victoria and Albert Museum collections description, this basket was a challenge to manufacture thanks to the limitations of porcelain and its tendency to warp and crack, especially in larger pieces like this one – 38 by 33cm with a height of 13.9cm (15 x 13 x 5.5in). As we already know, imitation Chinese-style scenes were very popular in domestic factories and this Worcester piece is no exception.

Royal Worcester, c 1755-57, Soft-paste
porcelain painted with underglaze blue
and moulded

Cream jug

This cream jug is of interest because of the somewhat organic and amorphous form it takes. The painterly surface decoration is clearly Chinese-inspired, but it also sits almost stiffly on the surface of the white jug form underneath. I love this contrast of the English-feeling form with the Chinese imitation surface pattern.

*At the time that this jug was made, much of Britain was drinking black tea, often sweetened with sugar, with milk or cream added. The lady of a well-to-do household would serve tea and coffee with a cream jug like this in the afternoon or after dinner. This jug would have cost more than the blue and white wares more common of the time because of the enamelled surface decoration. Enamelling takes additional firings to complete, whereas the blue and white would require far fewer firings.

*Royal Worcester, c.1753. Soft-paste
porcelain, painted with enamels*

The Music Lesson

As a potter it is no surprise that much of what I am attracted to are functional pots, which dominate my illustrations. Here I chose to share a porcelain figure to demonstrate the Chelsea Porcelain Factory's interest in mimicking the figurines that Meissen became so famous for.

✱ Chelsea porcelain figures are known for their exceptional quality and thanks to the use of soft-paste porcelain, they have a distinctive character. This figurine was inspired by an engraving of a François Boucher painting and the use of raised flowers here is an excellent representative of the trend of the time.

Joseph Willems Chelsea Porcelain Factory, c 1765. Soft-paste porcelain, painted in enamels and gilded

Cup and saucer

This cup and saucer illustrate a Japanese stylized plum blossom that the Bow manufactory was well known for early on. However, this is yet another example of an English riff on an Asian aesthetic, most likely inspired by objects popularly coveted. I particularly enjoy that these objects are a challenge to distinguish from similar pieces made in the Chelsea Porcelain Factory around the same time, because both factories were copying patterns from similar sources. The game of Chinese whispers with pattern continues …

*Near the end of 1867 drainage operations at the old Bow factory site revealed the foundations of the Bow kilns, together with a large quantity of 'wasters' and fragments of broken pottery, which helped to identify specific patterns as Bow rather than Chelsea. The houses nearby are still called 'China Row.'

Bow Porcelain Factory, c 1750.
Porcelain painted with enamels

Chapter 3
In the Studio

AN APPRENTICESHIP

My own studio practice and approach to making — much of my technical understanding of form and how to combine form with surface decoration — was honed during my apprenticeship to Vermont potter Miranda Thomas. Thomas had been an assistant to Michael Cardew — and Cardew was the first Western apprentice to Bernard Leach, the father of the twentieth-century studio pottery movement.

The shelves pictured here sat to the left of the wheel I worked at while an assistant at Miranda Thomas Pottery. As I threw pots, I looked up from time to time, and my eyes landed on the ceramics lining the walls in each room. I learned so much during this apprenticeship — from the pots I was surrounded by to the teachings passed on from master to apprentice in this Leach–Cardew tradition.

The story of studio potters today is rooted in the early twentieth-century studio pottery movement, which came after the height of domestic industrial manufacturing of tableware in Britain that took off after the discovery of domestic kaolin. So many of us potters have been directly influenced by Leach and Cardew and their philosophies about making pots.

Molly Hatch   A Passion for China

FAMILY TREE

SOETSU YANAGI
Japanese potter who championed Mingei movement in an effort to revive the handcrafted in Japan.

WILLIAM MORRIS
Father of the Arts and Crafts Movement in Britain.

BERNARD LEACH
Father of today's studio pottery movement in Britain. Brought Japanese Mingei philosophy to the West.

URANO SHIGEKICHI
Japanese master Kenzan VI potter.

SHŌJI HAMADA
Close friend to Bernard Leach, Japanese potter and Mingei philosopher. Came to Britain in 1920 to help Leach establish his pottery.

MICHAEL CARDEW
First British assistant to Bernard Leach. Established his own pottery in the UK as well as in Africa, with a long lineage of apprentices.

SETH CARDEW
Son of Michael Cardew. Continued to run Wenford Bridge Pottery in the Leach–Cardew tradition.

DAVID LEACH
Son of Bernard Leach. Potter who ran St Ives pottery after Leach stepped back from production.

MIRANDA THOMAS
One of Michael Cardew's last apprentices at Wenford Bridge Pottery. Worked alongside Seth Cardew and also apprenticed for Alan Caiger-Smith before moving to the USA to establish a pottery for Simon Pearce and then her own pottery in Vermont.

MOLLY HATCH
Studio potter, designer (and author), apprenticed with Miranda Thomas before starting her own studio.

ALAN CAIGER-SMITH
British studio potter. Colleague to Michael Cardew. Established Aldermaston Pottery and had over forty apprentices over his career.

STUDIO POTTERY IN THE WEST

At some time or another, just about every studio potter has come across Bernard Leach's iconic text, *A Potter's Book*. First published in 1940, this book is the core ideology of its author and became the essential reference for many generations of potters. As illustrated in the family tree, Leach's philosophy has been far-reaching, with a long legacy of apprentices and a pottery that is still producing wares in St Ives.

Leach's philosophic approach to making pots grew out of his interest in the British Arts and Crafts Movement combined with his time in Japan.

Living and teaching in Japan in 1916, Leach was introduced to Soetsu Yanagi, a Japanese scholar who championed the Mingei movement that revived crafts in Japan in the early twentieth century. Leach had studied etching at the London School of Art, but fell in love with the craft of pottery after attending a raku firing event. Leach's immediate excitement led him to secure a two-year apprenticeship with Urano Shigekichi, a Japanese master potter with the title Kenzan VI. It was during this apprenticeship that Leach learned to throw pots and apply surface decoration, as well as traditional firing methods.

Molly Hatch   A Passion for China

RAKU

Raku is a kind of traditional Japanese pottery. The first raku pots were made in the sixteenth century specifically for use in tea ceremonies. Raku pots are typically made using a hand-building technique rather than on the potter's wheel. They are fired to a low temperature and removed from the kiln while hot and cooled either in the air or placed into combustible materials like sawdust, creating a finished carbon surface that raku is best known for.

MINGEI   *'folk arts' or 'arts of the people'*

Mingei objects are anonymously made, crafted by hand, affordable for all, utilitarian and intended for daily use, regionally representative.

Mingei is a Japanese folk art movement founded by Soetsu Yanagi in the 1920s and 30s. Yanagi began the movement after a trip to Korea in 1916, where he was inspired by local ceramic traditions. Yanagi and two other Japanese potters — Shōji Hamada and Kanjirō Kawai — shared an interest in reviving the common Japanese Edo pottery that was quickly being replaced by manufactured goods, and the folk movement of Mingei was born. In 1936, the Japanese Folk Crafts Museum was established to aid in the preservation of the folk crafts of Japan.

In 1920, Leach returned to England from Japan to champion the Mingei approach. Valuing handmade and traditional craft over industrially manufactured objects, Leach laid a solid foundation for the revitalization of handmade pottery in the UK and the West. According to Leach, the character and spirit imbued in a handmade or handcrafted object cannot be successfully emulated in the manufactured.

Excited to earn a living as a studio potter and put his philosophy into practice, Leach worked hard to overcome many practical hurdles to set up his St Ives pottery studio with friend and colleague Shōji Hamada. Some of the biggest challenges Leach faced were procuring good clay for making his wares, getting his kiln functioning properly and the financial hurdles in keeping the pottery viable.

Before Hamada returned to Japan in 1923, a young Michael Cardew joined St Ives as the first British apprentice to Leach. Cardew was equally invested in Leach's philosophy of handmade traditionalism. Through teaching and writing as well as their studio apprenticeships, both men became influential icons within the ceramics field.

Leach stepped back from much of the pottery production prior to the Second World War, in order to dedicate his time to his writing and teaching, and his son David took over the running of St Ives. Leach's *A Potter's Book* was first published during this time, and his lectures and teaching led to the continuous publication of his book in multiple editions and solidified his legacy of influence on the studio pottery movement worldwide.

This little pot was the first
piece made by Bernard Leach
that I got to see in person

After three years of apprenticing Leach, Michael Cardew left St Ives and went on to re-establish a derelict pottery in Winchcombe, Gloucestershire. Working in the British slipware tradition local to the area, Cardew sourced indigenous clay to make his pottery, all true to the Mingei philosophic interest in making objects regionally.

Yanagi   Leach   Hamada

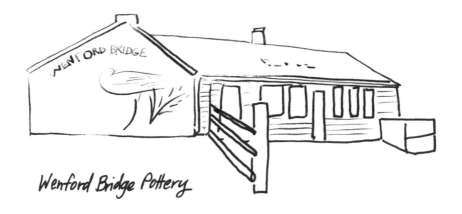

Wenford Bridge Pottery

In 1939, Cardew sold Winchcombe and moved to Wenford Bridge, St Breward, where he established an altogether new pottery with his young family. Cardew had dreamed of setting up a pottery in Cornwall and an inheritance allowed him to purchase an old inn and convert it into a pottery.

After completing colonial service in Ghana, from 1942 to 1948, where he taught ceramics at the Achimota School and nearby Alajo, Cardew returned to Wenford Bridge to make pots. In 1951, Cardew went back to Africa, this time to Nigeria as the pottery officer in the Department of Commerce and Industry. On his retirement from Abuja, Cardew again returned to Wenford Bridge. In later life, Cardew travelled extensively all over the world, lecturing and demonstrating. His autobiography, *A Pioneer Potter*, and book, *Pioneer Pottery*, are highly regarded and influential. During this time, Cardew took on many assistants who went on to establish their own successful potteries worldwide, working in the studio tradition that Cardew and Leach established.

Aldermaston Pottery

Miranda Thomas was one of Cardew's last assistants, from 1979 to 1981. With a focus on learning about form and surface, Thomas gained much technical knowledge and inherited her studio practice from Cardew in the Leach–Cardew tradition. You can see the aesthetic inheritance of an understanding of shape in particular in Thomas's pots.

It was also at Wenford Bridge that Miranda Thomas developed her iconic use of an iron-rich slip with a chun celadon glaze. At this time, Thomas lived in a nearby cottage and hunted rabbits and fished regularly. She dated a local farmer, and fell in love with the medieval idea of coexistence with animals. In an effort to make pots that were true to her, she began drawing the animals she knew and loved on her pots — from rabbits to fish, stags and songbirds.

Thomas went on from her apprenticeship to Cardew to be apprentice to Alan Caiger-Smith, from 1981 to 1983. As one of over forty apprentices over the years at the Aldermaston Pottery in the Berkshire village of the same name, she learned more about brushwork and surface decoration, driven always by the desire to successfully combine form and surface. Thomas carried forward her inherited knowledge from both these important apprenticeships when she established her own studio practice in Vermont.

Caiger-Smith wrote several books, including *Lustre Pottery* in 1985 and *Tin Glaze Pottery in Europe and the Islamic World* in 1973, establishing his academic mastery of the techniques Aldermaston pottery became so well known for. Meanwhile Thomas moved from Aldermaston to the US in 1984 to establish a pottery for glass artist Simon Pearce in Vermont.

Then in 1987, Thomas started her own pottery, also in Vermont, and in 2005 Thomas and her husband, furniture maker Charles Shackleton, merged his furniture with her pottery into one business called Shackleton Thomas. It is still in business today in Vermont. Thomas has been incredibly successful with her studio pottery. In addition to continuing the Leach–Cardew studio tradition with regularly taking on new assistants (myself included), Thomas has taught and lectured about her work and philosophy, including teaching at Harvard University for a time in the early 2000s.

Miranda Thomas runs her Vermont studio pottery in the tradition of Michael Cardew. I was fortunate to be there when Cardew's grandson Ara Cardew was working full-time in the pottery awaiting his green card. Starting my apprenticeship at the age of twenty-two, I knew very little of my great fortune in being hired as an assistant to a potter with such a direct lineage to Cardew.

Miranda Thomas Pottery

Today's studio pottery community reveres the pioneering philosophies of Leach and Cardew — often quietly upholding values and disciplines these potters laid foundations for almost a hundred years ago. While there are many who have pursued a life of making pots with success, the challenge is enormous and many studio potters today find it difficult to also maintain the Mingei philosophy. Studio potters face the challenge of making things by hand in a world that values the affordability of the manufactured object — but this is not a huge change from the motivation of the British Arts and Crafts Movement founders.

The fact that there is a drive and commitment to making the handcrafted pot even today proves there is still a place for the handmade. As you examine the ceramics in your cabinets and see the stories behind the objects you live with, ask yourself where the handmade and the factory-made might fit in — which do you reach for when you make your first cup in the morning? Which do you love for how it looks? Each has a place in our lives in its own way.

Staff of the Miranda Thomas Pottery in 2000. I am pictured to the far left with Miranda Thomas sitting on the bench to the left and Ara Cardew pictured to the far right leaning on the bench.

Plate

This Cardew plate is one of the
pots I most revered on the shelves
at Miranda Thomas's pottery. The
brushwork is clean and fresh — there
is a simplicity and an understanding
in the way the surface decoration
is applied that can only come with
repetition and familiarity with a design.
I work hard to achieve this same
quality of gesture in my own work.

This pot was made during Cardew's later life, when Miranda Thomas apprenticed at Wenford Bridge pottery in the late 1970s

Molly Hatch   A Passion for China

Jar

This was one of the many pots that
lined the walls of Miranda Thomas's
pottery in Vermont. I have come
to understand that this particular
double jar shape was inspired by one
originally by Shōji Hamada. The double
handles attach the two jars together,
but also visually reinforce the double
in concept. I remember being excited
to learn how to make the pillbox shape
of these jars — you throw a pot that
is fully closed and the lid is cut out of
the pot form. Wonderfully efficient and
simple, it's a jar that I still make in my
own studio practice.

This Cardew jar was from Miranda
Thomas's personal collection when
I was her apprentice

Coffee pot

This pot is made from the local Wenford iron-rich stoneware clay. Seth Cardew decorated it using a brush on top of the glaze with clay and iron cobalt pigments. The coffee pot was stacked in a saggar box and wood-fuelled in the Wenford kiln for about thirty-eight hours. This one sat on a shelf above the glaze mixing area in Miranda Thomas's pottery, so every time I mixed a glaze, the pot would watch over me. The integration of form and surface is lovely. The brushwork lands perfectly, accentuating the belly and emphasizing the form of the pot — it looks almost as though it is taking in a deep breath.

A coffee pot made by Seth Cardew,
Michael Cardew's son

Goblet

Caiger-Smith devoted his career to learning the secrets of the smoked lustrewares from the Middle East and Europe. He was well known for his surface decoration techniques and specifically his contemporary revival of smoked metallic lustres on tin-glazed wares. This goblet was hand-thrown and painted in alternate smoked copper (red) and silver lustres by Alan Caiger-Smith's assistant and studio manager Edgar Campden. It is a lesson in negative space and a simple build-up of pattern, using many elements of a brushstroke to decorate the surface.

An earthenware goblet from
Alan Caiger-Smith's pottery

Lustre plate

As an apprentice, I practised brushstrokes. I was given a special set of brushes as they wear to the artist's hand, especially when used in ceramics, as the brush tips are gently sanded from the rough surface of clay each time they are used. I learned an enormous amount about how to break up the physical form of a pot and calculate the rhythm of movement in a round object from my assistantship to Miranda Thomas. Caiger-Smith taught her how to wield a brush and approach surface decoration on a three-dimensional form with precision and elegance, allowing each brushstroke to be full of chance yet retain some control.

The flowing brushstrokes and controlled thick-to-thin elegance of Caiger-Smith's Aldermaston-style lustres introduced me to painting on pots

Molly Hatch   A Passion for China

Teapot

One of my favourite things about
Miranda Thomas's pots is her use of the
full space in the surface for decoration.
The way she carves the iron-rich slip
back to the stoneware clay below,
creating texture on the surfaces of her
pots as well as decorative contrast.
Here in this teapot, Thomas uses the
bunny motif to reflect her early days
as a potter's apprentice for Cardew,
living and working in Cornwall.

A Miranda Thomas teapot, evoking the
landscape of her Cornish apprenticeship

Platter

Thomas's carving of white slip over
stoneware clay came later on in
her career, and has since become
iconic of her wares. The white pieces
are fired in an electric kiln, making
for more consistent results in each
firing. I appreciate the softness of the
white and the way food is vibrantly
presented on this white pottery.

A carved white slip platter
by Miranda Thomas

Chapter 4

Popular Patterns

SHARED HISTORIES

Not long ago, I was visiting an aunt (one of my mother's sisters) for a family gathering. I explored her home for the first time, room by room, and when I found myself in her living room I suddenly had the feeling of being at home. I knew the objects here, because most of them had been my grandmother's before she passed. There were the French tobacco lamps on her side tables, a plate, a chest in lieu of a coffee table. This moment reinforced my interest in exploring the objects in my life, in our collective lives. It strengthened my thinking that our objects have their own personalities, their own histories. This is exactly why we keep them, it's why we love them and why they feel like home to us.

While I knew many of the stories of the ceramic objects I grew up with as they fit into my family's narrative, I have now learned an enormous amount about their role in our collective world history. Each piece of tableware has a history of its own, starting in the pottery or factory where it was made – yesterday or over 200 years ago. Its story continues when it becomes a part of our family life.

Pick up a teacup from your grandmother's shelf. Look more closely and you may see the back stamp from the factory that made it and you can begin to put together the larger story of that cup. Where was it manufactured? Who chose the design? Who else might have sipped from it? Ask your grandmother all about it. Where did that chip come from? Or those stains? Like scars on our bodies, these marks on our tableware add to the individual stories behind the objects we live with.

In this chapter I delve further into pattern. I know the individual flowers and birds, swirls and stars, of plates I ate from as a child have become part of my internal creative pattern bank. Which patterns do families across the English-speaking world share? And which potteries produced designs that have visually influenced whole generations? Here, I look at some of the most popular patterns sought out on the secondary market today, many of which you will recognize. Perhaps they trigger a memory — or maybe you are eating from these in your home today.

My hope is that, through the pages of this book, you can see how your story fits into the larger collective story of tableware. It may make you look twice at your cupboard of pots. And the next time you sit to eat a meal, you may pay a little more mind to the details of the dishes you are eating from, and wonder what stories they could tell if they could.

Lenox

The Poppies on Blue pattern was manufactured by Lenox for 23 years, from 1984 to 2007. Lenox is a New Jersey based manufacturer founded by Walter Scott Lenox initially as the Ceramic Art Company in 1889; in 1906 the name was changed to Lenox. In the early twentieth century, Tiffany & Company in New York made a large order, helping to establish Lenox as a leading American tableware manufacturer. Woodrow Wilson was the first of many presidents to order a service of Lenox tableware for the White House; others included FDR, Truman, Reagan, Clinton and Bush. While this pattern itself may not have made it into the White House, it was widely popular in the 1980s. The colour palette and brushwork reflect trends in home decor of the era, and I absolutely associate this pattern with visiting friends whose homes had what my family liked to refer to as the 'country duck' decor. A tableware pattern with a country charm made for daily use.

Lenox, Poppies on Blue,
1984-2007

Lipper & Mann

The original manufacturer of Blue Danube is thought to be Lipper International (then Lipper & Mann), with production beginning in 1951. There is much speculation about the production history of this pattern, with some thought that it has been in production for as long as 200 years. However, many pieces with this pattern have no manufacturer's mark on the back, making it very difficult to confirm. No matter where it was manufactured, its clear that the pattern is playing off our collective love for blue and white, and the Western value in Eastern motifs. Also, 'Blue Danube' is the common English title for the 1866 waltz by Austrian composer Johann Strauss II. The waltz refers to the blue of the Danube river. Perhaps one informs the other? Or a coincidence?

Lipper & Mann, Blue Danube,
1951

Royal Worcester

Introduced in 1961, this pattern was designed and produced in response to the increase of informal dining in Britain. Named after the local fruit-growing region, Evesham was Royal Worcester's bestselling pattern of the late twentieth century. Engraved lithograph stones printed the artwork onto the porcelain and hand-applied gilding finished the pieces. Much of Royal Worcester's tableware is still hand-decorated today. My mother has an oval covered dish in this pattern and she has always held it in high regard – as a result, I assumed it was more rare than it is. While made for more casual use, this pattern with its gold rim and detail is still more formal than everyday china.

Royal Worcester, Evesham Gold,
1961

Adams China

William Adams, founder of Adams China, worked for Wedgwood during the time the company developed its famous jasperware clay body, the result of more than 10,000 tests to get it right! Thanks to his work with Josiah Wedgwood, William Adams developed his own successful ceramic formula for an 'Ironstone' clay body. Adams Ironstone remained a secret formula in the Adams family for eleven generations. Although Adams China closed in the early 1990s, the products are still sought after. The Lancaster pattern was produced from 1969 through to 1998. Many of us are familiar with this hand-painted pattern thanks to its functional everyday value. Its country and folk references reflect the popularity of folk traditions of the 1970s and 80s.

Adams China, Lancaster,
1969-1998

Johnson Brothers

Johnson Brothers was founded in Staffordshire in 1883 by three brothers, Frederick, Henry and Alfred Johnson. Their products sold well in the United States after the fourth brother Robert (who was living in the US) joined the company. Transferware and flow blue porcelain were some of their most popular surfaces. Summer Chintz has long been a favourite Johnson Brothers pattern. Chintz is originally a reference to a kind of wood-blocked fabric patterns imported from India with designs featuring multicoloured flowers, vines and birds. The chintz patterns that we have come to love, like this, are typically European designs that are loosely derived from the original Indian fabrics.

Johnson Brothers, Rose Chintz-Pink,
1930-2003

Herend Porcelain

Herend Porcelain was founded in
1826 and began production in 1939,
in the village of the same name near
Budapest, Hungary. Stories vary as
to whether the bird-pattern porcelain
was ordered by the Rothschilds in
the 1850s or 1860, and whether it
was created for them or was already
in existence, but it was given the
name Rothschild decor in 1861. There
are twelve different motifs, each
symbolizing love and relationships.
Much later, Diana, Princess of Wales
chose a set with Rothschild decor
for her wedding reception.

Herend Porcelain, Rothschild Bird,
c. 1861

Gladding, McBean & Company

Gladding, McBean & Company began making clay products such as drainage pipes in 1875. In 1934 it introduced Franciscan Ware, a range of earthenware gifts and tableware – the Franciscan name symbolic of California, where the factory was based. The Franciscan Starburst collection, introduced in 1954, was designed by George James and reflected the futuristic post-war mid-century Modern aesthetic.

This tableware was at my grandparents' summer cottage on a lake. My father's mother was the typical American 1950s housewife. With strange salads consisting of Jell-O-moulded fruit and miracle whip dressings, my Grammie Dot represented a mid-century nuclear family lifestyle both in her personality and in her home aesthetic. I associate Franciscan Starburst with summer pancake breakfasts and beachy, sunny days.

Gladding McBean& Company,
Franciscan Ware, Starburst, 1954

Midwinter

Blue Dahlia was designed by Jessie
Tait and produced by Midwinter,
England, starting in 1972 and most
likely discontinued in the late 1970s.
Midwinter was a leading modern
tableware manufacture in 1950s–70s
Britain. Jessie Tait was the most prolific
in-house designer and she created
over 120 patterns for Midwinter. With
such a long history as an in-house
designer for Midwinter, the hand-
painted designs Tait produced were
iconic of a whole tableware period
in the mid-twentieth century.

Midwinter, Blue Dahlia,
1972-late 1970s

Pfaltzgraff

Pfaltzgraff was first made during the early 1800s, hand-thrown on a potter's wheel on a Pennsylvania homestead. Pfaltzgraff Pottery is one of the oldest family-owned pottery companies continuously producing in America. They began actively marketing in 1873 and also started using imported clay in an effort to improve quality of their wares. In 1895, Pfaltzgraff built a modern factory, streamlining manufacturing and began use of stencils to increase productivity. The Yorktowne pattern was based on original nineteenth-century Pfaltzgraff decoration and was introduced in 1967; it was named in honour of the first governing body in America formed in York, Pennsylvania, which made it America's true first capital city. While this pottery has a long production history, I really associate the popularity of this pattern and others in its family with the 1980s. The country folk reference suited my rural childhood and many of my friends' homes had patterns much like this on their kitchen table.

Pfaltzgraff, Yorktowne, 1967

Royal Copenhagen

The Blue Fluted pattern is known as
'Pattern No. 1' at Royal Copenhagen,
and has been in production for more
than 240 years. Royal Copenhagen
was founded in 1775 under the order
of the Queen of Denmark, and was
the first manufacturer to produce
porcelain in Denmark. The crown back
stamp with three waves below has
changed over time and can be used
to easily date each piece. The waves
represent the three Danish waterways:
the Oresund, the Great Belt and the
Little Belt.

Royal Copenhagen, Blue Fluted Half
Lace, c. 1775

Royal Winton

Summertime was introduced by Royal Winton in 1932. It was the most popular and widely produced Winton pattern until it was discontinued in 1960, due to the high production costs that came with the chintz style of decoration. Royal Winton was best known for their surface patterns, with more than sixty different chintz patterns introduced in the company history. While patterns like this, and the following by Spode, would have been considered functional, many of us likely never have actually eaten off them. I've always associated chintz patterns on dishes as being decorative objects, collectibles for display in the home. Perhaps the odd fancy chintz teacup and saucer was brought out at Granny's for a special tea, but most of the time I felt I wasn't meant to touch these beauties for fear of breaking them.

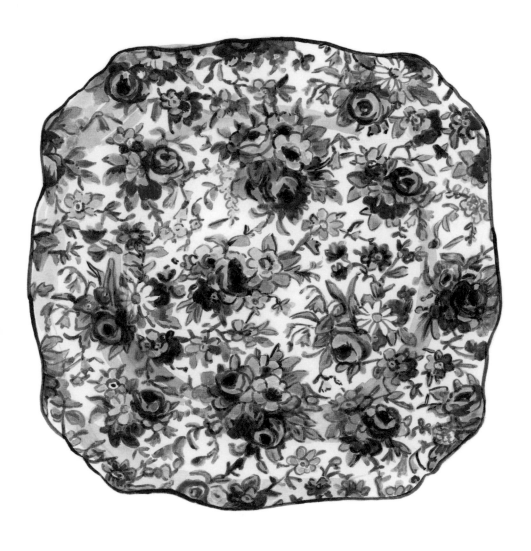

Royal Winton, Summertime,
1932-1960

Spode

Josiah Spode founded Spode pottery in 1770 at Stroke-on-Trent in Staffordshire. Rosebud Chintz was manufactured from 1954 to 1971. To create the surface pattern, the design is carved onto a copper plate. The pattern is then transferred to a piece of tissue paper with ceramic materials, and the coloured tissue is transferred to a blank plate. The plate is then immersed in water so the tissue is easily removed, leaving the surface pattern behind. The plate is then glazed and fired in a kiln, resulting in the finished product as we know it.

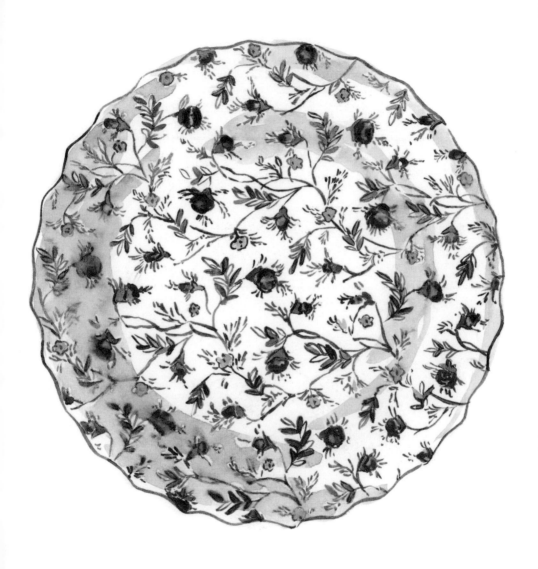

Spode, Rosebud Chintz,
1954-1971

A.J. Wilkinson, now Burgess and Leigh

Burleigh Blue Calico is a transfer pattern first produced in 1960 by A.J. Wilkinson of Burselm, Staffordshire. The inspiration is said to be a nineteenth-century calico, a type of cloth known for its all-over floral print. It was first sold in America, but was so popular it was soon distributed more widely, including in Habitat in the UK. From 1968 Burgess and Leigh, also of Staffordshire, took over manufacturing, and they still sell it today. My love of calico is similar to my love of chintz – the tight all-over floral pattern that is often found in quilting fabrics is well suited to tableware.

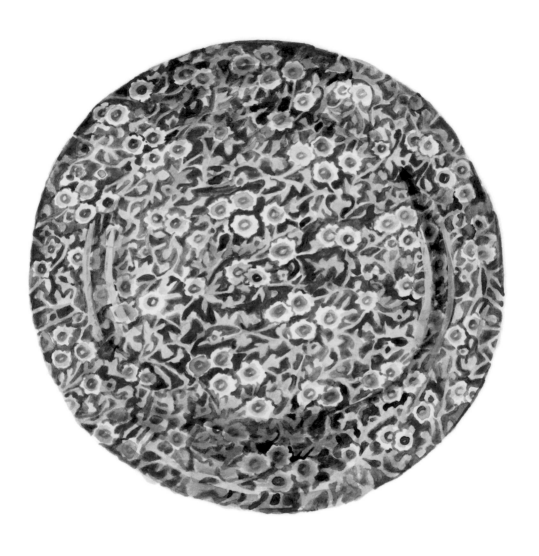

A.J. Wilkinson, Burleigh Blue Calico,
1960

Wedgwood

The Williamsburg Potpourri pattern
was manufactured for forty-two years,
from 1956 to 1998, by Wedgwood. Based
in England, Wedgwood patterns are
typically only manufactured for ten to
twenty years, making the Williamsburg
Potpourri pattern unique in its longevity.

Wedgwood, Williamsburg Potpourri,
1956-1998

A.G. Richardson, Cobridge

Crown Ducal Bristol Pink was made by A.G. Richardson of Tunstall and Cobridge in Staffordshire, and was first released in 1931. The name Crown Ducal was used from 1916, and became a well-known producer of chintz pattern dishes. A.G. Richardson closed in 1974. I love the look of this pattern, it is such a great example of the traditional UK transferware, the surface decoration done with traditionally printed decals from engraved rollers. A similar pattern is still being produced by the Burleigh manufactory in the UK. Listed as the Pink Asiatic Pheasants pattern, it also comes in blue and plum, and it is still printed with the same type of engraved rollers that it was originally.

A.G. Richardson, Cobridge,
Crown Ducal, Bristol Pink, 1931

Acknowledgements

A Passion for China is the result of the generosity of many people. First, to my editor Hannah MacDonald, for coming to me with a book concept that resulted in such an amazing journey through my own story and ceramic history alike. I am deeply grateful for your persistence and patience as the book came together. To all of those who have worked on this book with me at September Publishing, particularly Charlotte Cole and book designer Sandra Zellmer: you made visual sense of each chapter that exceeded expectations.

I am indebted to my family for opening their cupboards, sending photographs, patiently answering all of my questions about our family and for being encouraging of my sharing our story. I am delighted to honour my maternal grandmother, Myma, in this book; her objects do such a wonderful job of representing her. Working on gathering my favourite objects from Myma's home felt like reclaiming a piece of them and committing them to memory. I am particularly thankful to my mother, Camilla Roberts, my aunts, Kaela Farber and Tisha Lewis, and my uncle, Josh Metcalf, for sending photographs and stories. Thank you to my cousin, Cassidy Metcalf, for sending photos of Miranda Thomas's pottery studio. I love that you are a working as a potter for Miranda as I once did.

I owe much of the third chapter to my mentor and friend Miranda Thomas. Thank you for the lovely afternoon teas and long studio visits. My understanding of your heritage and my lineage as a potter has greatly deepened thanks to working on this book and your willingness to recount your past with such generosity. Thank you for permitting photographs of your pottery and your studio to be included in this book, it wouldn't be the same without these peeks into the past.

This book wouldn't have been possible without calling on a long list of resources. I am so appreciative of the

Metropolitan Museum of Art, the Victoria and Albert Museum and the Musée des Arts Décoratifs for maintaining such incredible resources both in their museums and in their collections online. I am indebted to two curators at the Museum of Fine Arts in Boston for their additional information about objects in their collections: Thomas Michie, senior curator of decorative arts and sculpture, and Laura Weinstein, Ananda Coomaraswamy curator of South Asian and Islamic art.

Much of the research done for this book came from articles and online resources thanks to the help of researcher Kelly Shetron, including the websites of many of the manufacturers and potteries still producing their wares today. I am very appreciative of access to history so directly from the source, specifically the Leach Pottery and the Royal Copenhagen websites. Replacements, Ltd has been an enormous wealth of knowledge about tableware patterns and their histories and an incredible reference throughout writing this book; I can't thank you enough for sending me all that you did.

In addition to online resources, I relied heavily on several publications that I recommend for further reading. Edmund de Waal's book *The White Road* helped inform much of the historic timeline of the move of porcelain from the East to the West. *The Willow Pattern Story* by Allan Drummond, *Dish: 813 Colorful, Wonderful Dinner Plates* by Shax Riegler, *The Potter's Art* by Garth Clark and *Dinnerware of the 20th Century: Top 500 Patterns* by Harry L. Rinker.

Finally, thank you, dear reader, for confirming my notion that there is more to our tableware than meets the eye, that there is bigger story waiting to be told.

Photo credits

Page 16, family portrait, mid-1980s, photo by a family friend Johanna Woodcock • page 19, Myma's old living room, family photo, unknown photographer, permission given to publish by my aunt Kaela Farber • page 37, portrait of Myma smoking, by Molly Hatch in 1994 • page 60, Molly at Pompeii in 2001, taken by another tourist • page 62, photo of the view outside of the top floor of the gardens at the Louvre in Paris, 2016, by Molly Hatch • page 85, Fonthill Vase, photo courtesy of the National Museum of Ireland • page 108, Molly at the potter's wheel in 2000, photo by Autumn Cipala • page 109, pot shelf above studio door, 2017, photo by Sophie Shackleton • page 121, Miranda Thomas pottery staff, 2000, photo taken by timer!

About the author

Molly Hatch is the daughter of a painter and a farmer. She spent her childhood on an organic dairy farm, where she created art from an early age. She received her BFA from the Museum School in Boston in 2000 and after several ceramic residencies and apprenticeships in the US and abroad received an MFA in Ceramics from the University of Colorado. Her career has led to collaborations with institutions such as the Museum of Fine Arts in Boston, the Metropolitan Museum of Art, the Clark Art Institute and the High Museum of Art Atlanta. She has collaborated on product design and illustration widely, across the design and publishing industries, as well as institutions such as the Victoria and Albert Museum, London.

10 9 8 7 6 5 4 3 2 1

First published in 2017 by September Publishing

Design by Sandra Zellmer

Printed in China on paper from responsibly
managed, sustainable sources
by Everbest Printing Co. Ltd

ISBN 978 1 910463 33 8

September Publishing
www.septemberpublishing.org
www.mollyhatch.com